I HATE® STANFORD

303 Reasons Why You Should, Too

Crane Hill
PUBLISHERS
BIRMINGHAM, ALABAMA
1996

I HATE® STANFORD

303 Reasons Why You Should, Too

by Paul Finebaum

CRANE HILL
PUBLISHERS

Printed in the United States of America
Published by Crane Hill Publishers
Many thanks to John Carrigan.

Library of Congress Cataloging-in-Publication Data

Finebaum, Paul, 1955-
  I hate Stanford: 303 reasons why you should, too / Paul Finebaum.
    p.   cm.
  ISBN 1-57587-034-7
  1. Stanford University — Football — Miscellanea. 2. Stanford
University — Sports — Miscellanea. I. Title.
GV958.S7F55   1996
796.33'263'0979473--dc20   96-19814
                                                            CIP

10   9   8   7   6   5   4   3   2   1

I HATE STANFORD

I Hate Stanford Because…

1. John McEnroe learned his manners at Stanford.

2. The most humiliating moment in the history of Stanford football was losing to lowlife East Carolina in the Liberty Bowl.

3. Ted Koppel went to Stanford—nothing else needs to be said.

4. Herbert Hoover also went to Stanford–*for sure* nothing else needs to be said.

5. Ted Danson's acting career does not speak well for Stanford's school of fine arts.

6. Ken Kesey had the Stanford faculty in mind when he penned *One Flew Over the Cuckoo's Nest.*

7. The performances by the Stanford marching band in the infamous Cal game has served as a model for Stanford defenses for more than a decade.

8. The Cal kick returner passed through the Stanford marching band so quickly and effortlessly that one advertising agency is considering using the footage for a laxative commercial.

9. Tiger Woods is a Stanford student but only on days that it rains.

10. Ted Leland became Stanford's athletic director in a very unique way—nobody else applied for the job.

11. Also, Leland told schools officials that he was related to Leland Stanford—and they believed him.

12. The top 10 reasons Ty Willingham got the head football coaching job are: Stanford was looking for someone cheap after Bill Walsh.

13. Willingham promised to get to a bowl game in 5 years.

14. Willingham reminded Ted Leland of Denzel Washington.

15. Willingham correctly named the president and vice president of the United States.

16. Willingham knew that Frankfort—not Louisville—is the capital of Kentucky.

17. Willingham told the Stanford search committee privately that he thought Bill Walsh was a geek.

18. Willingham promised the Stanford search committee that he could get them Charles Barkley's autograph.

19. Willingham promised that his athletes would graduate—as long as they didn't have to take any hard courses.

20. Willingham also promised that he would line the field at Stanford Stadium.

21. Willingham didn't ask for a contract.

22. When he's recruiting, coach Mike Montgomery plays up the "fabulous climate" Stanford has to offer.

23. Coach Montgomery also reminds potential recruits that Stanford provides one of the healthiest college social environments.

24. Once in a while coach Montgomery gets around to mentioning that Stanford has won the prestigious Sears Cup twice.

25. When incoming Stanford freshmen were asked what the Sears Cup is, the top 5 responses were: An athletic supporter worn while shopping at Sears.

26. A new kind of coffee served at Sears.

27. A special bra size sold only by Sears.

28. The third leg of the Triple Crown.

29. The award given for the lowest grade-point average.

30. Coach Montgomery utterly confuses his players with his strange tic-tac-toe—they don't understand how there can be so many Xs and Os.

31. Coach Ty Willingham is often criticized for letting the team play with action figures during games.

32. The flags at Stanford are flown at half-mast on Squeaky Fromme's birthday.

33. The top 10 bumper stickers seen on the Stanford campus are: The only thing worse than having influence is having none.

34. Poverty sucks.

35. Ralph Nader for president.

36. Don't blame me, I voted for Huffington.

37. Save the Cardinal.

38. Cal is for the underprivileged.

39. Honk if you had a class with Ted Kaczynski at Cal.

40. Bi American.

41. Go Giants and take the 49ers with you.

42. Free Ty Willingham.

43. It's a little-known fact that Stanford's sports teams are named in honor of gridiron legend Cardinal John O'Connor.

44. When a reporter pointed out that Tyrone Willingham was actually Stanford's third choice to replace Bill Walsh, Willingham replied, "That's okay— I was my wife's fourth choice."

45. Cardinal basketball players have a lot on the ball— unfortunately it's not usually their hands.

46. Cardinal basketball players wear Birkenstocks to cut down on the irritating squeaking noises during games.

47. The Cardinal football team is so bad that when Stanford students hear the phrase "college bowl game" they assume it refers to an academic contest.

48. Stanford's defense is so bad that when they accidentally have 12 players on the field the referees feel so sorry for them that they don't throw the penalty flag.

49. Stanford athletes don't take academics too seriously, but quarterback Tim Carey does use a protractor when he diagrams plays in the dirt.

50. Despite being so close to the center of the computer industry, the biggest technological innovation to come out of Stanford in the last 10 years is the clapper.

51. Stanford's motto is Latin for "Born to Lose."

52. The students are just damn smart.

53. The top 10 guesses for what the S on the Stanford football helmet stands for are: Stupid.

54. Surly.

55. Sullen.

56. Stuck-up.

57. Sassy.

58. Saucy.

59. Smelly.

60. Stinky.

61. Soused.

62. Smashed.

63. "I just can't figure out why everyone in the Pac-10 runs all over us," said one Stanford nose tackle as he sat eating his tofu and alfalfa sprouts.

64. Charles Schwab learned how to do things cheap at Stanford.

65. Hal Ramey is living proof that anybody can broadcast college football on radio.

66. So is Kris Atteberry.

67. Stanford's water polo team's winning percentage has dropped off sharply since Pac-10 officials stopped letting them take horses into the pool.

68. Tara Van Derveer's 5 favorite moments of the 1996 Olympic Summer Games were: Getting into an arm-wrestling match with Charles Barkley.

69. Having free Coke 'round the clock.

70. Getting to meet those cute Italian wrestlers.

71. Leaving Atlanta—what a dump!

72. Getting Bob Costas's autograph.

73. The most exciting thing to happen during a Stanford football game last season was an earthquake.

74. President Gerhard Casper thinks he is related to Casper the Friendly Ghost.

75. The captain of the Cardinal cheerleading squad is nicknamed "Will Rogers" because she never met a man she didn't like.

76. William Rehnquist went to law school at Stanford.

77. That's one reason the legal system in this country is so messed up.

78. John Steinbeck learned all about the dark side of human nature at Stanford.

79. "Breaking a fingernail" is a common reason to be excused from Cardinal football practices.

80. Sportscasters covering the Stanford football team often say, "I'm sorry, folks, I've got a correction for all of you watching at home–that play was *not* shown in slo-mo."

81. A strong wind could knock over Stanford's defensive line.

82. Ted Koppel's top 10 hobbies while he was a student at Stanford were: Interrogating his journalism professors until they cried.

83. Trying to get dirt on the homecoming queen.

84. Doing Mamie Eisenhower impersonations at frat parties.

85. Bragging to students that he was going to be the next John Cameron Swayze.

86. Sitting for hours on end in front of a full-length mirror and practicing being a TV interviewer without moving anything but his lips.

87. Racing classmate Phil Knight down the street in P.F. Flyers.

88. Getting into mud-wrestling matches with Sandra Day O'Connor.

89. Running around campus yelling that Walter Cronkite was a washed-up hack.

90. Sneaking around the president's mansion and going through old garbage.

91. Practicing his Huntley-Brinkley impersonation while alone in the shower.

92. Stanford professors give oral exams that allow students to shout out responses as if they were contestants on *Family Feud.*

93. Some Stanford professors have responded to recent salary cuts by simply making stuff up for their lectures.

94. In the late 1980s, the Stanford student body considered changing the football team's name to the Dancing Raisins.

95. Former student Ken Kesey's book *The Electric Kool-Aid Acid Test* was an accurate portrayal of freshman orientation at Stanford.

96. Stanford students love to compare their school with Harvard, but they don't like to admit that the school's biggest similarity is the common tradition of losing on the gridiron.

97. Stanford's fight song is "Send in the Clowns."

98. It takes 2 Stanford students to change a lightbulb–
1 to change the bulb and the other to say loudly that
he did it as well as a Cal student.

99. John Elway learned all he ever needed to know
about losing big games from his days at Stanford.

100. During a heated exchange, one Stanford student
was heard to shout, "What do you mean it's *bad acid?*
It worked great in my car battery!"

101. Surprisingly enough, offering high school recruits discounts on the latest computer software has not given Stanford the top recruiting classes in the Pac-10.

102. What do the dark side of the moon, a dentist's office, and the Rose Bowl have in common? All of them are places no Stanford football player has ever visited.

103. Stanford's baseball coach likes to take the team to San Francisco to see the Giants play.

104. Unfortunately all the players have learned from the field trips is a few new techniques for scratching themselves.

105. Cardinal football players rarely write more than a paragraph on an essay test with adding "uh-huh."

106. Quarterback Tim Carey is more successful throwing passes off the field than during games.

107. Stanford's new policy of recycling unsold basketball tickets has already saved 25 acres of forest.

108. The only thing Stanford leads the Pac-10 in is groin pulls.

109. The 10 sportswriters Ty Willingham hates the most are: Scott Ostler.

110. Joan Ryan.

111. Gwen Knapper.

112. John Crumpacker.

113. C. W. Nevius.

114. Dwight Chapin.

115. John Curley.

116. Mark Purdy.

117. Ray Ratto.

118. Art Spander.

119. Every Stanford professor's dissertation ends with the word "maybe."

120. The Stanford basketball team often blows off games near the end of the season in hopes of picking up a lottery draft pick.

121. Due to lack of funding, Stanford's giant telescope has been replaced by a kaleidoscope pointed at an overweight gentleman dressed as the Big Dipper.

122. The top 10 ways to start a fight at Stanford are: Round off pi after only 2 decimal points.

123. Ask the woman seated in front of you at Stanford Stadium to please remove her rainbow wig so you can see the game.

124. Misquote dialogue from *Star Trek: The Next Generation.*

125. After knocking something off a table, shrug your shoulders and say, "Don't blame me, it's San Andrea's fault."

126. Dart back and forth through the Stanford marching band while remaining untouched.

127. Loudly question the healing powers of crystals.

128. Politely ask a professor to stop propositioning your girlfriend.

129. Walk up to Tim Carey and say, "I thought you were just great in *Ace Ventura.*"

130. Talk trash about the size of another guy's hard drive.

131. Pop a paper bag and watch the noise send Stanford's defensive line scurrying off like kittens.

132. The Cardinal football players prefer Birkenstocks over traditional cleats.

133. A Hollywood director has cast one of the Cardinal football players for the leading role in *Babe Part II: The College Years.*

134. Starting quarterback Tim Carey has an unfair advantage over his contenders–he has taught the Cardinal center how to talk through his butt.

135. The Cardinal basketball team turned down a big contract to do a Wheaties commercial and opted to do a bran muffin ad instead.

136. The Cardinal football team is introduced on the field with music by John Tesh.

137. The football team therapist keeps telling the players to act less defensively.

138. The Cardinal offensive line tries not to "block" the true feelings of their opponents.

139. Coach Tyrone Willingham has been advised by his therapist to get out of his codependent relationship with his team.

140. Stanford students' top 10 career goals are: To be Michael Irvin's attorney.

141. To be chairman of Hewlett-Packard.

142. To be Bill Gates's second wife.

143. To inherit Apple Computer.

144. To be the editor of *Leather and Lace*.

145. To marry Willie Brown.

146. To go 10 rounds with Barbara Boxer.

147. To have a McDonald's server spill hot coffee on you.

148. To become Paul Finebaum's book publisher.

149. To marry Tiger Woods.

150. The Stanford business school offers a course called "Racketeering, Tax Evasion, and Screwing the Middle Class."

151. Quarterback Tim Carey works as a cable guy in the off-season.

152. The best part about going to a Stanford football game is it's never hard to find a parking place.

153. The average ACT score for incoming freshman coed is 31–which is also the average number of sexual partners to date.

154. Coach Tyrone Willingham said that sportswriter Paul Finebaum reminded him of Moses. Finebaum thought it was a compliment until Willingham added, "Yeah, every time he opens his mouth the bull rushes."

155. Stanford has a bowl tradition of staying home.

156. The following books are required reading for Stanford business majors: *Line, Symbol, and Pie—Oh, Those Colorful Graphs!*

157. *Selecting the Clip-On Power Tie That's Right for You.*

158. *Elderly Employees Easier to Bully and Other Effective Hiring Strategies.*

159. Funny-Looking People on Foreign Money: A History.

160. Make Big $$$ Selling Your Unused Prescriptions.

161. The Flat Tax has nothing to do with the chest size of most Stanford coeds.

162. Stanford is one of the few schools in America where the dorms offer room service.

163. And maid service.

164. And all the cheap women you can find.

165. The Cardinals mistook the word "turf" for "surf" and were last seen heading for the beach.

166. Coach Ty Willingham's favorite saying is "Let's just all get along with each other."

167. The New Age Cardinal athletes drink herbal tea instead of Gatorade.

168. The Cardinals use a Dumb and Dumber offense.

169. Cardinal animal rights activists keep protesting "Dead Animal" football games.

170. Cardinal players are taught to be sensitive to their opponents.

171. The top 5 things to do at Stanford on Saturday night are: Drive to Berkeley.

172. Drive to San Jose.

173. Drive to Pebble Beach.

174. Drive to San Francisco.

175. Drive to Sacramento.

176. When the Cardinal football players found out they were going to the Liberty Bowl, they wanted to know whether the water in it was blue or Clorox clear.

177. Listening to Troy Clardy of KZSU is a doctor-approved treatment for insomnia.

178. Stanford students think that a panty raid is roach spray for underwear.

179. In keeping with California's environmental laws, Stanford has become a totally biodegradable institution.

180. Stanford's fans are usually too busy trying to save the opposing team's faux-animal mascot to watch the game.

181. Most Stanford students think South America is where Alabama is located.

182. Coach Ty Willingham doesn't think holding should be a penalty if the other guy is hurting inside.

183. Coach Willingham's top 10 reasons why going to a Stanford football game is better than having sex are: Nobody has to perform well.

184. There's usually less noise.

185. You don't have to worry about how you smell.

186. You don't have to act like you're enjoying it.

187. You don't have whisper.

188. It lasts longer.

189. Most Stanford men get more for their money at a football game.

190. You won't have to see your wife for 4 hours or so.

191. There's no reason to fake a headache since the game will give you one.

192. There's little chance of procreation.

193. The Cardinal football players got "tongue itch" when their jockstraps got mixed up with their mouth pieces.

194. A number of Stanford students found out the hard way that they couldn't get high smoking AstroTurf.

195. Cardinal basketball players enjoy disrupting games by sucking the air out of the ball to get a quick buzz.

196. Coach Mike Montgomery has developed a unique and effective language to communicate with his players—it consists of different sequences of grunts and whistles.

197. A recent survey showed that 60% of the Cardinal football players are making straight As, and most are doing quite well on the rest of the alphabet too.

198. Most Stanford students believe that nondairy creamer comes from dehydrated cows.

199. Most of them also think that low-fat milk comes from skinny cows.

200. Paul Finebaum's column is required reading for all Cardinal players. Audiotapes are provided for those who can't read.

201. The top 10 reasons incoming freshmen chose to attend Stanford are: Cal was full.

202. Cal Tech's requirements were to stiff.

203. They wanted to attend a school where football team wouldn't be a distraction.

204. They wanted to attend a school where basketball wouldn't be a distraction.

205. The men didn't want sexy women distracting them in library.

206. They wanted to attend a school where they wouldn't have to waste time waiting in line for football tickets.

207. They wanted to experience Palo Alto.

208. Most women thought it might lead to a possible date with Tiger Woods.

209. Stanford is easier to spell than many other California schools.

210. Their parents made them go to Stanford.

211. When the police stopped coach Mike Montgomery for a traffic violation, he said, "I know I was driving on the wrong side, but the other side was full."

212. Cardinal football players spend 20 minutes at a time staring at orange juice cans that say "concentrate."

213. Bleached blonds at Stanford are nicknamed Frosted Flakes.

214. Cardinal football players like to play David & Goliath with their jockstraps.

215. Stanford graduates make excellent daytime talk-show guests.

216. Seniors at Stanford spend a fortune on dentures and Depends.

217. Stanford students believe that Diet Coke will help them lose weight and get high at the same time.

218. President Gerhard Casper has gotten so old that his thoughts have drifted from passion to pension.

219. Stanford coeds think that dry cleaning involves vacuuming clothes.

220. Cardinal football players think their teammates are pretty.

221. At Stanford SEX is a Greek organization.

222. The only thing easier than a class at Stanford is getting a coed to say, "Just do it."

223. Many Stanford students think *The X-Files* is a TV porno show.

224. Cardinal football players sit down to pee.

225. Many of the Cardinal cheerleaders, however, lift their leg to pee.

226. Stanford students air their dirty laundry by taking a walk outside.

227. The top 10 radio and television personalities Mike Montgomery hates the most are: Bob Murphy.

228. Hal Ramey.

229. Dan Fouts.

230. John Evans.

231. Jackie Brambles.

232. Gary Radnich.

233. Martin Wyatt.

234. Troy Clardy.

235. Brian Phelps.

236. Mark Thompson.

237. A dope ring is 5 Cardinals standing in a circle.

238. Cardinal players think that speed dial is a soap.

239. Athletic director Ted Leland is so cheap that he once punished his children for buying all-day suckers at 5 p.m.

240. If ignorance is bliss, the Cardinal football coaches must be the happiest people on earth.

241. Before Cardinal grads have sex, they make sure the stork has taken a birth control pill.

242. The Cardinal media relations staff members never let the facts interfere with their opinions.

243. Coach Mike Montgomery should try to get ahead—he certainly could use one.

244. Coach Ty Willingham makes at least one big mistake every day—he gets out of bed.

245. President Gerhard Casper talks so much that people get hoarse just listening to him.

246. Cardinal football players are usually disagreeable, repulsive, and obnoxious—and those are their good points.

247. Broadcaster Hal Ramey could talk his head off and never miss it.

248. The top 10 comments recently overheard outside The Quad are: "Oh, Tiger's tail is sooo cute."

249. "Really, I always thought Bill Walsh was cute for an old coot."

250. "Wouldn't you give anything to rub that fuzzy wuzzy beard of Dan Fouts."

251. "Hey, anybody want to go swim nude tonight in the pool at White Plaza?"

252. "I'm so made at Daddy. He sold our Gulfstream, and now, we have to fly to the Super Bowl in that cheap little Citation."

253. "My mother dated Tom Watson in college. He was a much better putter back then, according to Mom."

254. "I know he smells and passes gas, but his daddy owns the lodge at Pebble Beach."

255. "Excuse me, but does anybody have a spare condom. I'm running low and it's only Friday."

256. "I met the cutest girl the other day—on the Internet."

257. "Of course, not—why would anyone waste time going to a Stanford football game?"

258. When he was asked to name the 10 biggest thrills of his life, coach Ty Willingham responded: Being mentioned in Paul Finebaum's *I Hate Stanford* book.

259. Being interviewed by the Fabulous Sports Babe.

260. Getting to caddy for Tiger Woods.

261. Having Sandra Day O'Connor pinch his butt during homecoming weekend.

262. Having Phil Knight tell him once to "Just do it."

263. Getting Warren Christopher's autograph.

264. Sparring with Jack Palance.

265. Reading the *San Jose Mercury Press* sports section without using his hands to point.

266. Sitting at ringside during the Ultimate Fighting Challenge.

267. Being kissed on the lips by senator Diane Feinstein.

268. Broadcaster Bob Murphy's brain has paused permanently for station identification.

269. One of coach Ty Willingham's main goals is to establish a program that is "consistent"–Cardinal fans hope he means "consistent in winning."

270. Athletic director Ted Leland is always trying—very trying.

271. Coach Ty Willingham's character and leadership are his trademarks—now he just needs to work on winning.

272. Many of Stanford's professors complain that whenever they get truly brilliant idea, the nurses won't let them have a pencil to write it down.

273. Before registration, Stanford students are required to be up-to-date on all of their immunizations–including rabies.

274. Most Stanford students think that a microwave is how they're supposed to cheer at low-attendance games.

275. Coach Ty Willingham often gets his playbooks mixed up with his coloring books.

276. Stanford students think that an instant camera must be stirred into boiling water.

277. Cardinal football players think that a book is something that is thrown at people.

278. Someone always has to tell the Cardinal football players when the game is over because they don't know how to tell time.

279. President Gerhard Casper boasts that Stanford is a place "where studies blossom and the minds move"–blossom into what and move where is debatable.

280. Stanford grads make excellent daytime girlie-show hosts.

281. Stanford athletes think vowels are something that digest the food they eat.

282. Animal testing stopped at Stanford after the football players complained about the pain.

283. Everybody tests positive for everything at Stanford.

284. If the Cardinal football players were required to take a math class at Stanford, "1st and 10" might make some sense to them.

285. Big muscles, little brains–and that's just the women.

286. Cardinal players get really upset when a game is scheduled at noontime on Saturday because it makes them miss all the good cartoon shows.

287. *Baywatch* is not just a TV show for Stanford students–it's a way of life.

288. Jon Bon Jovi's motto is "If Stanford kids keep buyin' them, I'll keep makin' them."

289. California animal rights activists believe the Cardinal football players have the right *not* to play if they don't want to.

290. *Cheers* star Ted Danson left Stanford before he graduated—evidently the classroom was not a place "where everybody knows" his name.

291. Mike Montgomery is sick and tired of hearing about Stanford football considering that his basketball program is considerably better.

292. Sigourney Weaver prepped for her role in *Alien* by dating Stanford frat boys.

293. A Stanford coed sold her computer because it missed a period and she thought it was pregnant.

294. Stanford administrators believe that searching to know something is much more valuable than actually knowing something.

295. Sally Ride was spaced out at Stanford.

296. Roy Dolby got so tired of listening to his professors babble at Stanford that he invented a noise reduction system.

297. Stanford encourages deviant behavior by telling its students that challenging assumptions is reason to celebrate.

298. To boost ratings next season, play-by-play Stanford football games will be done by John Tesh and Elfi Schleigel.

299. Keith Peters of the *Palo Alto Weekly* is all the more reason newspaper writers should be required to attend high school.

300. John McEnroe perfected his court etiquette while he was at Stanford.

301. The Bill Walsh tradition continues—no coaching, no winning, no problem.

302. After losing to USC, one Stanford player scowled, "Aaaah, don't worry about it guys—it's all just one big popularity contest anyway."

303. The biggest seller at the campus bookstore this year will be *I Hate Paul Finebaum* by Tommy Charles.